Community Helpers and BUILDERS

# Building Places to Shop

Written by
William Anthony

Designed by
Amy Li

KidHaven PUBLISHING

Published in 2023 by KidHaven Publishing,
an Imprint of Greenhaven Publishing, LLC
29 East 21st Street
New York, NY 10010



**Edited by:**
Robin Twiddy

**Designed by:**
Amy Li

**Cataloging-in-Publication Data**

Names: Anthony, William, 1996-.
Title: Building places to shop / William Anthony.
Description: New York : KidHaven Publishing, 2023. | Series: Community helpers and builders | Includes glossary and index.
Identifiers: ISBN 9781534541092 (pbk.) | ISBN 9781534541115 (library bound) | ISBN 9781534541108 (6 pack) | ISBN 9781534541122 (ebook)
Subjects: LCSH: Shopping--Juvenile literature. | Stores, Retail--Juvenile literature. | Community development--Juvenile literature.
Classification: LCC TX335.5 A58 2023 | DDC 381'.1--dc23



Manufactured in the United States of America

CPSIA compliance information: Batch #CSKH23: For further information contact Greenhaven Publishing LLC, New York, New York at 1-844-317-7404.

Please visit our website, www.greenhavenpublishing.com. For a free color catalog of all our high-quality books, call toll free 1-844-317-7404 or fax 1-844-317-7405.

Find us on

**Photo Credits** Images are courtesy of Shutterstock.com. With thanks to Getty Images, Thinkstock Photo and iStockphoto.

Recurring images – ONYXprj (builders), Elenamiv, sidmay (blue background), Guiyuan Chen (wood background), art4stock (push pins), ag1100 (crumpled paper). Cover – LightField Studios, p4–5 – Nina Buday, p6–7 – Nolte Lourens, Maria-Cezara Panaite, Rawpixel.com, Sergiy Bykhunenko, p8–9 – KK Tan, p10–11 – Glinskaja Olga, mimagephotography, SnvvSnvvSnvv, Impact Photography, p12–13 – Tropper, p14–15 – Dmitry Lobanov, Hryshchyshen Serhii, PV productions, p16–17 – MIA Studio, p18–19 –Sorbis, Dean Drobot, Anatoliy Karlyuk, Katt_Parrot.

# Contents



Words that look like <u>this</u> can be found in the glossary on page 24.

# Meet the Local Area Builders

Hello! We're the Local Area Builders. We help communities by building important things in their local area. This map is quite empty, isn't it? Someone will need somewhere to shop soon, I'm sure!

# New Building Needed:

## Something for Fashion

I want to go shopping for clothes, but there's nowhere to go! I love <u>fashion</u> and dressing in the coolest clothes. Can we build a clothing store?

– Jamie, age 6

That didn't take long! Let's get going on our first job!

# Clothing Store

A clothing store is where people go to buy the things they wear. In a clothing store, you could buy dresses, shirts, shoes, or even a funky hat.

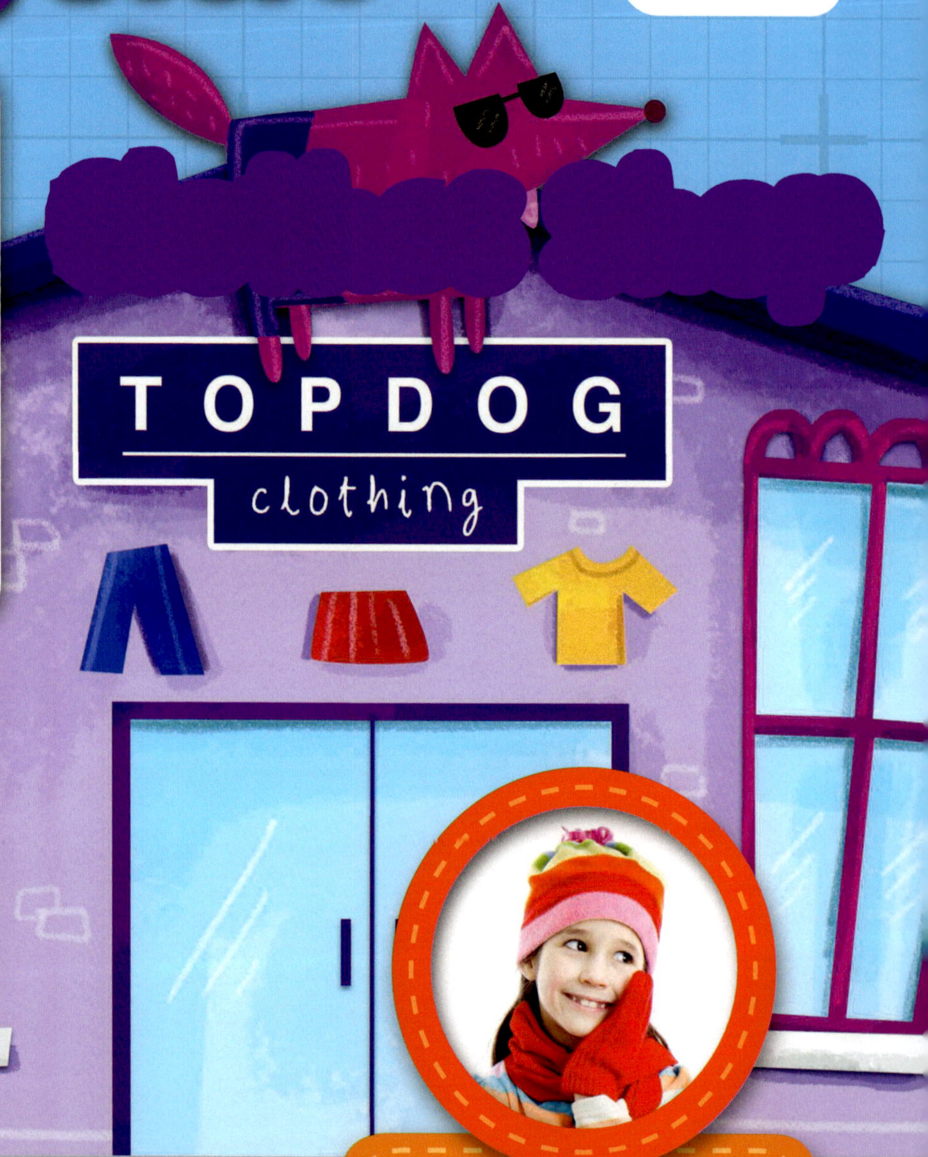

I love wearing bright clothes to stand out!

In a store, we use money to buy things.

I like to wear sweaters and jeans to school!

Many people wear different styles of clothing. Every style is different and great in its own way. Whatever style you like is great if it makes you happy!

# Map Update

That clothing store will keep everyone looking great! I think we should build two or three clothing stores, so there are lots of styles to choose from.

# New Building Needed:

## Something Artsy

I love painting, drawing, and making things – anything to do with art! But I have run out of paint and paper! Could we build a store where I could get these things?

– Sara, age 5

Of course we can. Let's get building!

# Arts and Crafts Store

An arts and crafts store is a place where you can buy materials for art projects. You can buy things such as paper, pencils, paint, glue, and many more artsy items!

I can make lots of different things by folding paper. It is called origami.

Art can be a fun hobby. What hobbies do you have?

I paint how I feel. If I'm happy, I use bright colors!

Art can be anything you want it to be. It might be a dot on a page, a swirl of colors, or a big painting of someone's face. All art is different and good.

# Map Update

This place is going to look amazing! An arts and crafts store will help people with their hobbies. Maybe we could even have an art show one day!

# New Building Needed:

## Something for Food

Cooking is one of my favorite hobbies. It's fun to do, and when you're done you get a tasty treat! I need a place to get **ingredients**. Can you help?

– Ben, age 5

# Supermarket

I like the section with all the candy! Who wouldn't?

A supermarket is a store where you can buy all kinds of food, from vegetables to candy. Supermarkets are usually very big stores.

Always stay with an adult when you visit a supermarket. It is easy to get lost!

Supermarkets don't just sell food. They sometimes sell things like birthday cards, stationery, and video games.

# Map Update

That was a big building – maybe the biggest we've ever built! I think we should add a smaller food store too, for when people only need one or two things.

# New Building Needed:

## Something Fun

Toys are the best. They are the best of the best. But there's nowhere in the local area where I can get new ones! Can we build a fun toy store?

– Cho, age 5

This should have been the first store we built! Let's get going!

# Toy Store

Toy stores are full of fun and wonder. They are packed with toys, games, puzzles, and more. Toy stores might have new toys or toys from many years ago.

Dolls are great because you can act out stories with them.

I love doing puzzles because they are a challenge.

Some toy stores have toys that you can try out in the store. The people that work there might show you how a toy works and let you play with it.

# Our Local Area

That toy store will give us kids a place to have lots of fun! The map looks much better now. Maybe one day we could build a big shopping center.

Our work here is finished. This local area has many places to buy things and explore different hobbies. It's time to go and build something else. Great job, everybody!

# Your Local Area

It's time to try creating a local area yourself! Get a piece of paper and draw a map like the one on page 4.

What's in your local area? Are there toy stores and supermarkets?

Think about your local area. Draw all the places where you can buy something on your map. Or you could make one up and go completely bonkers! It's up to you!

What's in your made-up local area? What about a shop made from candy or a place you can buy a pet dinosaur?

# Glossary

| | |
|---|---|
| communities | groups of people who live and work in the same place |
| fashion | a popular way of dressing |
| hobby | an activity that somebody does for fun |
| ingredients | things that are used to make food |
| materials | things from which objects are made |
| money | something used to pay for things |
| projects | things that require careful work over a long time |
| shopping center | group of stores in one area, sometimes in a very large building |
| stationery | things that are used for writing or drawing |
| styles | ways that people are dressed |

# Index

Community Helpers and BUILDERS

## Titles in This Series

Building Places to Explore

Building Places to Learn

Building Places to Play

Building Places to Shop

ISBN: 9781534541092
6-pack ISBN: 9781534541108

9 781534 541092

KidHaven PUBLISHING